EXPLORATION THROUGH THE AGES
THE TRAVELS OF MARCO POLO

Richard Humble

Illustrated by
Richard Hook

Franklin Watts
London · New York · Toronto · Sydney

© 1990 Franklin Watts

First published in Great Britain
in 1990 by
Franklin Watts
96 Leonard St
London
EC2A 4RH

First published in the USA by
Franklin Watts Inc
387 Park Avenue South
New York, N.Y. 10016

First published in Australia by
Franklin Watts Australia
14 Mars Road
Lane Cove
NSW 2066

UK ISBN: 0 86313 875 6

A CIP catalogue record for this book is available from the British Library.

Designer: Ben White

Illustrations: Richard Hook, Hayward Art Group

Photographs: Bodleian Library 4, 5, 14, 17, 23; John Pilkington 11.

Words in bold appear in the glossary.

Printed in Belgium

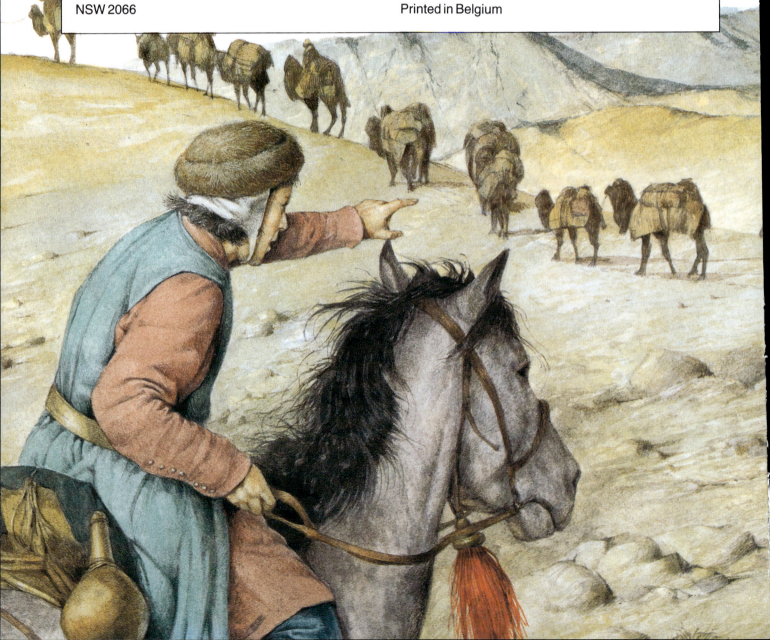

Contents

Empire of the Mongols	4	The Buddha's tooth	20
Eastward bound	6	With India's pearl fishers	22
Bandit attack!	8	Return by sea	24
The "Roof of the World"	11	The travellers return	26
Across the Gobi	12	"Marco Millions" tells his story	28
At the court of the Great Khan	14	Glossary	30
The wonders of Cathay	16	Timechart	31
The land of pagodas	18	Index	32

Empire of the Mongols

The world has never seen anything like the conquests of the Mongols, 700 years ago. United and led from victory to victory by their great leader, **Genghis Khan**, the hard-riding armies of Mongol warriors overthrew every great power between China and eastern Europe.

When Genghis Khan died in 1227, the Mongol conquests continued under his sons. By 1241 the Mongols had taken southern Russia and were swarming west through Poland and Hungary. But when they heard of the death of Ogadai Khan, third son of Genghis, the Mongol generals headed home to elect the next "Great **Khan**". Europe was therefore saved from Mongol rule.

Under the greatest of the Mongol khans, **Kublai** (1215–94), the Mongol Empire reached its widest extent. Though the **khanates** often fought among themselves, all submitted to Kublai's authority as Great Khan.

Kublai proved that the Mongols were far more than ferocious warriors. A wise ruler, he cared for the welfare of his millions of subjects. As the new Emperor of conquered China – his favourite land – he preserved the wonderful buildings, art and learning of Chinese civilization.

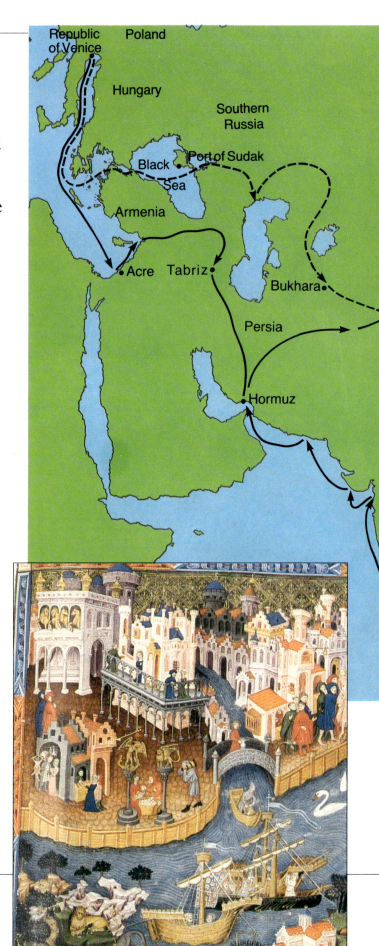

▷ From the English manuscript "Book of the Great Khan", an early edition of Marco Polo's travels of about 1400. This view shows Venice, Marco's birthplace, with the domed Cathedral of St Mark's and the splendid Palace of the Doges, the dukes who ruled the Republic of Venice and its sea-trading empire.

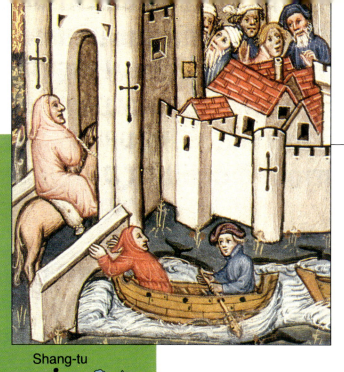

◁ "The great river Balacian", from the "Book of the Great Khan". This was another name for the upper stream of the River Oxus, which the Polos followed on their journey east through the Central Asian mountain province, known as Badakhshan.

But Kublai was also deeply curious about the world outside the Mongol Empire. He was especially interested in Christian Europe, which the Mongol leaders before him had spared. He welcomed and gave his full protection to all Europeans hardy enough to make the long and difficult land journey, over 4,000 km (2,500 miles), to China.

The first of these visitors were Christian missionaries, Friar John in 1245 and Friar William in 1253. However, after the missionaries came European merchants who were eager to make money by trading with the new power in the Far East.

The most daring and energetic of these merchants came from the Republic of Venice, the richest trading nation of the Western world. By the late 1250s, Venice had trading posts all along the east Mediterranean coast and at the port of Sudak on the Black Sea. It was from Sudak, in 1260, that the Venetian merchant brothers Niccolo and Maffeo Polo headed east on a trading journey, destined to carry them to the court of Kublai Khan himself.

△ By the year 1260, the vast empire of the Mongols stretched across Asia from the China Sea to the plains of southern Russia. It was from the port of Sudak on the Black Sea (*upper left*) that the Venetian merchants Niccolo and Maffeo Polo set off on their first journey to the court of Kublai Khan in Cathay (China).

5

Eastward bound

It took the brothers over four years to reach China, or **Cathay** as they called it. This comes from the Mongol-based name *Khitai*. After four years they were brought before Kublai Khan in his capital city of Khanbalig, known today as Beijing.

Niccolo and Maffeo remained in Cathay for a whole year as honoured guests of Kublai. He asked them many questions, especially about the Christian Church and its head, the Pope in Rome. Finally, Kublai asked the brothers to return to Italy on a special mission for him. Kublai wanted some of the holy oil from the Church of the Holy Sepulchre, Christ's burial-place in Jerusalem. And he wanted the Pope to send no less than 100 Christian missionaries to spread the Gospel in Cathay.

The Polos set out for home in 1266 as ambassadors of the Great Khan. Apart from rich presents they also carried his passports: tablets of gold measuring 30 by 8 centimetres, engraved with Kublai's order for the carrier to be given all the food, shelter and transport he needed on pain of death. They reached Acre, on the Mediterranean coast, in April 1269.

Bad news was waiting for them. Pope Clement IV had died the year before and the cardinals in Rome could not agree on whom to elect as the new Pope. The Polos decided to wait for a new Pope to be elected. However, after waiting for two years, they could stay no longer. It was time to return to Cathay. They sailed for Acre from Venice in 1271, and with them they took Niccolo's son, Marco. He was then 17 years old.

◁ The triangular lateen sails of a Venetian merchant ship swell to the wind as Niccolo, Maffeo and Marco Polo set sail from Venice. Their first goal was Palestine, to fetch the sacred oil from the Holy Sepulchre Church in Jerusalem, which Kublai Khan had requested.

Bandit attack!

The three Polos were still in the Holy Land when they heard that a new Pope, Gregory X, had at last been elected. He could not provide the 100 missionaries for which the Great Khan had asked, but he sent a letter of goodwill for the Polos to take to Kublai. The new Pope also ordered the two leading friars in the Holy Land to go to Cathay with the Polos. They also travelled to Jerusalem and obtained a flask of the holy oil before beginning the long, overland journey to the East.

But no sooner had all these preparations been made than the Polos heard of a new threat: an invasion of the Holy Land by a raiding army of **Mamelukes** out of Egypt, posing great danger to all travellers to the East. It was too much for the two friars, who refused to go on. Niccolo, Maffeo and Marco made the brave decision to return to Cathay anyway to explain the failure of their mission to Kublai in person.

So began the first of the wonderful journeys described in Marco Polo's book

of *Travels*, one of the most famous travel stories in history. Marco's account makes it clear that his father and uncle had decided to make up for lost time by travelling through Armenia and Persia to Hormuz on the Persian Gulf. From there they could make better speed by travelling further east by ship.

Like other merchant traders, the Polos sought safety in numbers by travelling with a group, or **caravan**, but as they approached Hormuz across the plain of Rudbar, the Polos' caravan was attacked by one of the most feared bandit tribes of the region: the **Karaunas**.

These hard-riding robbers liked to make use of the sudden "dust fogs", stirred up by the hot winds of the Rudbar area. Nervous travellers, as Marco notes in the *Travels*, therefore believed that the Karaunas had the power of raising magic mists to help their attacks. The Karaunas attacked during one of these fogs. The caravan scattered in panic and Niccolo, Maffeo and Marco were forced to ride for their lives. Pursued by the Karaunas, the Polos were not safe until they were behind the stout walls of the nearest town.

◁ Yelling battle cries and storming out of the dusty gloom of a "dry fog", a war party of the dreaded Karauna bandits attacks the Polos' caravan as it heads for the port of Hormuz. Against such a surprise attack, which sent the caravan scattering in panic, the only way out for the Polos was to ride for their lives, seeking safety behind the walls of the first fortified town they could find.

9

The "Roof of the World"

The Polos were citizens of one of Europe's greatest seafaring nations – Venice – and one look at the ships they found at Hormuz was enough for them. The Arab boats of Hormuz were ramshackle coastal fishing craft, clearly unfit for any kind of long ocean voyaging. There was nothing for it but to change their plans and complete the return journey to Cathay by land.

From Hormuz their route lay north to Kerman and north-east through Shibarghan to Balkh, Talikhan, and Ishkashan; climbing, always climbing through the green mountain province of Badakshan until they reached the remote Plain of Pamir, the "Roof of the World", 4,750 metres (15,600 feet) above sea level.

Marco was lucky not to see the plain in the icy desolation of winter. Instead he was impressed by the grass: "a lean beast grows fat here in ten days", he noted. Everywhere they saw the large sheep of Pamir with their huge, curling horns which are still known, in Marco's honour, as *Ovis Poli*, "Polo's sheep". Their horns and bones lay everywhere. Travellers piled them into high cairns, or heaps of stones, to mark the track in the winter snows. Wandering shepherds used the horns and bones to make fences, which would protect their flocks from wolves. They also made drinking-bowls out of the great horns.

It took the Polos twelve days to trek across the lofty emptiness of the Pamir plain. They saw no birds and not a single human habitation. And they noticed in wonder that even fire seemed to have changed its nature. It was impossible to build a good blaze against the icy chill of the nights. Their fires provided little heat and made it virtually impossible to boil water for cooking.

Today we know that the fires did not burn well because of the Plain of Pamir's great altitude (or height) above sea level, where there is less oxygen in the air. This was not known until many centuries after Marco Polo's death. He thought it was due to the intense cold of the night and just another of the many wonders he saw during his travels.

◁ In the cold, thin air of the lofty Pamir Plain, the Polos stare in disbelief at a camp-fire that gives little heat for warmth or cooking.

△ Marco's description of the great sheep of Pamir resulted in his name being given to the species. Even today, sheep are still important to the people.

Across the Gobi

When the Polos started on their journey downhill from the "Roof of the World", they entered a region which Niccolo and Maffeo knew from their first journey to Cathay. This was the province of Turkestan with its five major cities: Kashga, Khotan, Pen, Charchan and Lop. At Lop they prepared for one of the biggest ordeals of the land route to Cathay: the crossing of the Gobi, one of the world's greatest deserts.

Few Europeans today, let alone of 700 years ago, are familiar with the dangers of desert travel, and Marco's account of the crossing of the Gobi tells of its vastness. "This desert is reported to be so long that it would take a year to go from end to end; and at the narrowest point it takes a month to cross it. It consists entirely of mountains and sand and valleys. There is nothing at all to eat."

Fortunately the trade route to Cathay across the Gobi was well established, and the crossing of caravans from Lop to Suchow took about 30 days. At Lop, the western starting-point, Marco noted that,

"Travellers who intend to cross the desert rest for a week to refresh themselves and their beasts. At the end of the week, they stock up with a month's provisions for themselves and their beasts. Then they leave the town and enter the desert."

To stray from the caravan meant a lingering death in the desert from sunstroke and thirst. All travellers were warned not to heed the "visions" (heat-haze and mirages) and "spirit voices" (strange sounds made by the blowing of the wind over dry, shifting sands) which often lured careless travellers to their doom.

Marco did not know the real reasons behind these illusions but he knew that the dangers existed. The Polos listened to the warnings, stayed close to the caravan and came safely through the Gobi.

▽ As the long caravan plods wearily across the burning wastes of the Gobi, Marco gets his first experience of a desert mirage. Caused by the shimmering of air in intense heat, mirages were feared as "visions" that lured the unwary.

At the court of the Great Khan

Once the Polos emerged from the Gobi Desert, they found themselves in western Cathay's Tangut province. Now the long outward journey was nearly over in all but name as they travelled through cities familiar to Niccolo and Maffeo from their first visit: Suchow, Sinju, Kalachan and Tenduc.

The deeper the Polos advanced into Cathay, the greater were the honours and respect earned for them by Kublai's golden passports. At Chagan-nor, they were entertained at one of Kublai's favourite palaces. The hunting-grounds there were vast and deer roamed freely. Messengers had galloped east to inform the Great Khan of the coming of the Polos, and he was delighted at the news. Kublai at once sent out a royal escort to meet the Polos and bring them with honour to his summer palace at the city of Shang-tu.

Marco looked in wonder at Kublai's summer palace, where the Great Khan spent the months of June, July and August each year. It was built like a giant tent of sliced bamboo; Marco described it in his book *Travels*,
"...the interior all gilt and decorated with beasts and birds of very skilful workmanship. It is reared on gilt and

▽ Like most European rulers of the age, Kublai Khan had a passion for hunting and Marco was astonished at the size of the Great Khan's packs of hounds. Here the "Book of the Great Khan" shows Kublai hunting deer, boars and bears with his beloved hounds.

△ With watchful guards preventing them from touching the threshold (believed by the Mongols to be bad luck), the three Polos are made welcome at Kublai Khan's beautiful Summer Palace in the city of Shang-tu.

varnished pillars, on each of which stands a dragon, entwining the pillar with his tail, and supporting the roof on his outstretched limbs."

Kublai welcomed Niccolo and Maffeo warmly, as old and honoured friends who had been away too long. He was delighted with their gifts, especially the holy oil from Jerusalem, and he was not offended that they had failed to bring any of the Christian missionaries for whom he had asked.

Then Kublai noticed young Marco and asked who he was. "Sire," said Master Niccolo, "he is my son, and your true servant." Kublai smiled graciously, "He is heartily welcome", he replied.

15

The wonders of Cathay

As an honoured guest at the court of Kublai Khan, Marco was the first European to report in detail on the wonders of Cathayan civilisation, which Kublai had so carefully preserved after the Mongol conquest.

The son of a merchant-trading family, Marco was amazed by the use of paper money, instead of gold and silver. This was unknown in the Europe of his day, and for many centuries to come. Stamped with the Great Khan's seal, these paper banknotes were used to buy up all the gold, silver and jewels that came into Kublai's realm. Refusal to accept the banknotes in exchange for goods, precious metals or jewels was punishable by death.

Another wonder to Marco was the use of

coal fuel in Cathay: "stones that burn like logs", as he put it. "If you put them on the fire in the evening and see that they are well alight, they will continue to burn all night, so that you will find them still glowing in the morning."

Marco found that coal was used everywhere in Cathay. He noted that it was more efficient than wood, and he

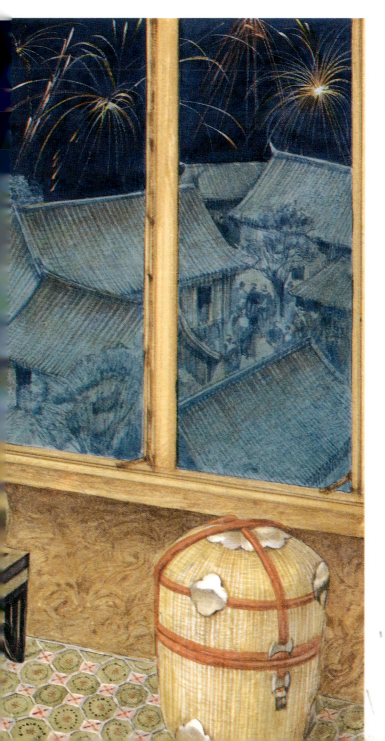

◁ Another marvel which Marco found in Cathay was the use of banknotes instead of coins. Here he tries to understand how mere "pieces of paper" can buy the same amount as gold and silver.

△ From fact to fiction. In later years, the wonders that Marco saw for himself on his travels were turned into fabulous legends. One legend told of these grotesque man-monsters, said to inhabit the land of India.

decided that the people preferred to use coal because of their passion for hot baths. They took baths at least three times a week and every day in winter at public bathhouses. Such a custom had been unknown in Europe since the fall of the Roman Empire 900 years before.

Marco was equally astonished by the Imperial Post. There were three classes: "second" was a foot-runner service, "first" was delivered faster, on horseback, and "top priority" using a despatch rider and a relay of fresh horses, could deliver a message 300 miles away within 24 hours!

The land of pagodas

Kublai Khan liked the young man who had come to his court with his old friends, the Polos. He also greatly respected Marco's ability to remember details and describe them clearly. Kublai needed to know about life and events in the distant parts of his vast empire. He therefore persuaded Marco to make several long journeys in his service, reporting back to the Great Khan on everything he saw.

Marco's first journey in Kublai's service was south to the Cathayan border province of Kara-jang (modern Yunnan province, China). Ruled over by one of Kublai's sons, Essen Temur, Kara-jang was the base for the latest Mongol war of conquest against the Kingdom of **Mien** (modern Burma).

In 1272, while the Polos were still beginning their long journey east to Cathay, the King of Mien had rashly attacked the Mongols in Kara-jang, only to be totally defeated in battle. Marco was therefore not only the first European to visit Burma: he went there at a time when the country was occupied by a Mongol army. The country was beaten and subdued, but with the glories of its past still undamaged.

Marco visited the Burmese capital of Pagan on the River Irrawaddy, and he marvelled at its beautiful pagoda towers. Two of these, built in memory of a former King of Mien, were particularly beautiful,

▷ As a friend and trusted official of Kublai Khan, Marco made several journeys through the Great Khan's lands. One of these visits was to Burma. Here we see Marco viewing the superb pagodas, plated with gold and silver, in the Burmese capital city of Pagan.

as Marco recorded: "One of these towers was built of fine stone and then sheeted with gold as thick as a finger, so completely covered that it appeared to be made only of gold. The tower was circular, and all around it were hung small gilded bells which tinkled whenever the wind blew through them. The other tower was plated with silver, but built to the same plan and to the same size as the golden one."

The Buddha's tooth

Apart from several land journeys through Cathay, Tibet and Burma, Marco made at least two long sea voyages in the service of the Great Khan. These were to the island of Ceylon (known now as Sri Lanka), in 1284.

Kublai was very interested in the world's leading religions – Christianity, Judaism, Buddhism and Islam. He wanted to know about each religion's God, "so that I may be sure of doing honour to

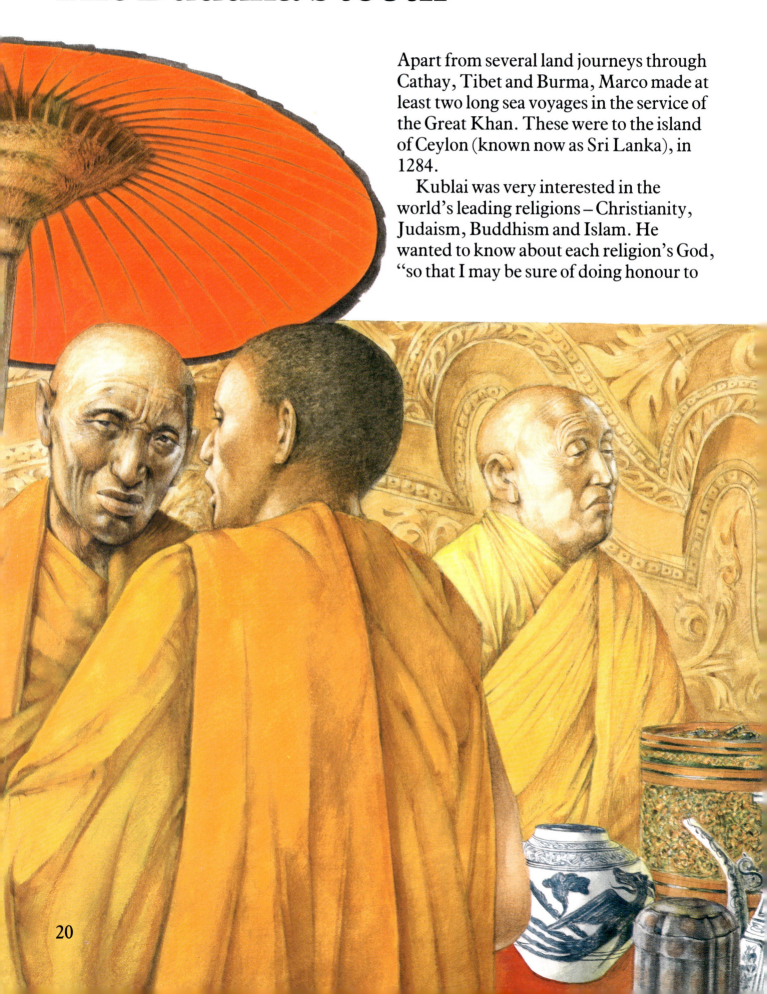

him who is greatest in heaven and truest, and to him I pray for aid." Kublai already had holy oil from Jerusalem and he heard that the island of Ceylon held two famous Buddhist relics – the tooth and begging-bowl of Buddha himself. He sent Marco to Ceylon with an immense treasure and told him to buy both relics from the Buddhist monks.

Marco saw many more wonders during his long sea voyage down the Cathayan and Vietnamese coasts to Java, westward through the Straits of Singapore, and finally across the Bay of Bengal to Ceylon. He drank the wine of the toddy-palm, ate the "flour" collected from beneath the bark of the sago tree and marvelled at the strength and heaviness of ironwood.

Marco was deeply impressed with his visit to Ceylon and the legends connected with Adam's Peak, the mountain in the centre of the island. "It is said that on the top of this mountain is the monument of Adam, our first parent." The bargaining with the Buddhist monks went well, and they agreed to sell the relics Kublai wanted. The price was high; "what they cost me in treasure amounted to no small sum", confessed Marco. But when the relics were brought back to Khanbalig, Kublai "welcomed them with great joy and great ceremony and great reverence".

But Marco had failed to buy another item highly valued by Kublai in Ceylon. This was the world's biggest ruby, a treasure of the ruling kings of Ceylon: "about a palm in length and of the thickness of a man's arm, it is the most brilliant object to behold in the world, free from any flaw and glowing red like fire". The monks refused to sell this at any price.

◁ Marco has voyaged from Cathay to the island of Ceylon to purchase the Tooth of the Buddha for Kublai. Here two Buddhist monks discuss the price in treasure which Marco has just offered. After much bargaining he succeeds in buying the Tooth, but does not succeed with the world's biggest ruby.

With India's pearl fishers

After completing his mission to Ceylon, Marco crossed to the southern mainland of India, where he visited the great province of Maarbar, today the Indian province of Tamil Nadu. Here he found that the richest local industry was pearl fishing, and he described how it was done in words still as fascinating for us to read today as they must have been for Kublai Khan to hear.

The pearl fishing on the Maarbar coast was strictly controlled by the King of Maarbar, who demanded high taxes from the pearl fishers. Pearl fishing was a skilled and dangerous job and so merchants had to hire divers and their boats. A group of merchants agreed to be partners and they provided a ship large enough to tow several small boats from which the pearl divers worked.

"The men in the little boats, who have been hired by the merchants, jump overboard and dive into the water, sometimes 3 fathoms down, sometimes 4, sometimes as much as 10 (about 18 metres). They stay under as long as they can. When they can endure no longer, they come to the surface, rest a short while and then plunge in again; and so they continue all day. While they are at the bottom, they gather there certain shells which are called sea oysters. In these oysters are found pearls, big and small and of every variety. The shells are split open

and put into tubs of water. The pearls are embedded in the flesh of the shellfish. In the water this flesh decays and takes on the appearance of white of egg. In this form it floats to the surface, while the pearls remain at the bottom. That is how the pearls are gathered. And I assure you that the quantities gathered are beyond counting. For you must know that pearls gathered in this gulf are exported throughout the world, because most of them are round and beautiful."

Marco also noted the custom of paying one pearl in twenty to the Brahman priests whose task was to protect the divers from shark attacks by offering special prayers throughout the day.

△ How the "Book of the Great Khan" interpreted Marco's detailed account of pearl fishing from the Maarbar Coast in southern India.

◁ Marco watches keenly as a pearl diver breaks the surface, clutching a net bag crammed with oysters. In the nearest boat, men are separating the pearls by soaking the oysters in tubs of water. When the flesh rots and floats to the surface, the pearls are left undamaged at the bottom of the tubs.

Return by sea

So the years passed for Marco, with repeated journeys and visits to gather information in his long and eventful service to Kublai Khan. Far less is known about what Niccolo and Maffeo did during Marco's travels, but they were certainly trading and building up a big fortune with Kublai's goodwill.

All in all, the three Polos spent seventeen years in Cathay, and despite the richness and honour of their life they naturally became homesick. "Time and again", says Marco, "we asked the Khan to give us leave to depart, but he was so fond of us and so much enjoyed our company that nothing would persuade him to give us leave."

Then came the day when messengers arrived from Arghun, the Mongol Khan of **Persia**. Arghun's queen had died, and he was asking Kublai to send a princess of the royal family to become his second queen. Kublai chose the 17-year-old Princess Kokachin, "of great beauty and charm", and he prepared a royal escort to take her to her future husband. Persia was many miles to the west of Cathay and the journey would be a long one. But by the time the escort was ready to leave with the Princess, another war between the Mongol Khans had closed the land route from Cathay to Persia.

◁ As the Polos prepare to embark in their fleet of junks (Chinese sea vessels) for the long sea voyage home, a big man-carrying kite is flown to see if the omens are favourable for a lucky voyage.

Marco had just returned from another sea voyage to India, and so the Polos seized their chance. They persuaded the escort to ask Kublai if they could take the Princess west by sea. Kublai reluctantly agreed.

They sailed from the great sea port of Cathay: Zaiton (modern Hsia-men), in a fleet of fourteen ships brought together on Kublai's orders. The ships Marco described were far bigger than anything built in Europe at the time. They had 4 masts with as many as 12 sails, crews of up to 260 seamen, stout wooden hulls divided into water-tight compartments that would control flooding in the event of shipwreck or accident, and at least 60 passenger cabins.

A strange ritual took place before Cathayan ships set sail on long voyages: the launching of a huge man-carrying kite. If it soared cleanly upwards, the voyage would be lucky; if it failed to climb, the ship would stay in port.

The travellers return

From Marco's account in his book *Travels*, the return voyage from Cathay to Persia was one of the most dangerous he ever made. Apart from the crews of the ships, 600 people sailed from Cathay, of whom 100 were women who attended Princess Kokachin. However, only eighteen men reached Persia safely, among whom were the three Polos. All the others, and one of the women, had been killed on the voyage.

The trouble seems to have started on the island of Sumatra, where the fleet had to spend five months waiting for fair weather before sailing on to the west. "Here", says Marco, "we landed from our ships and, for

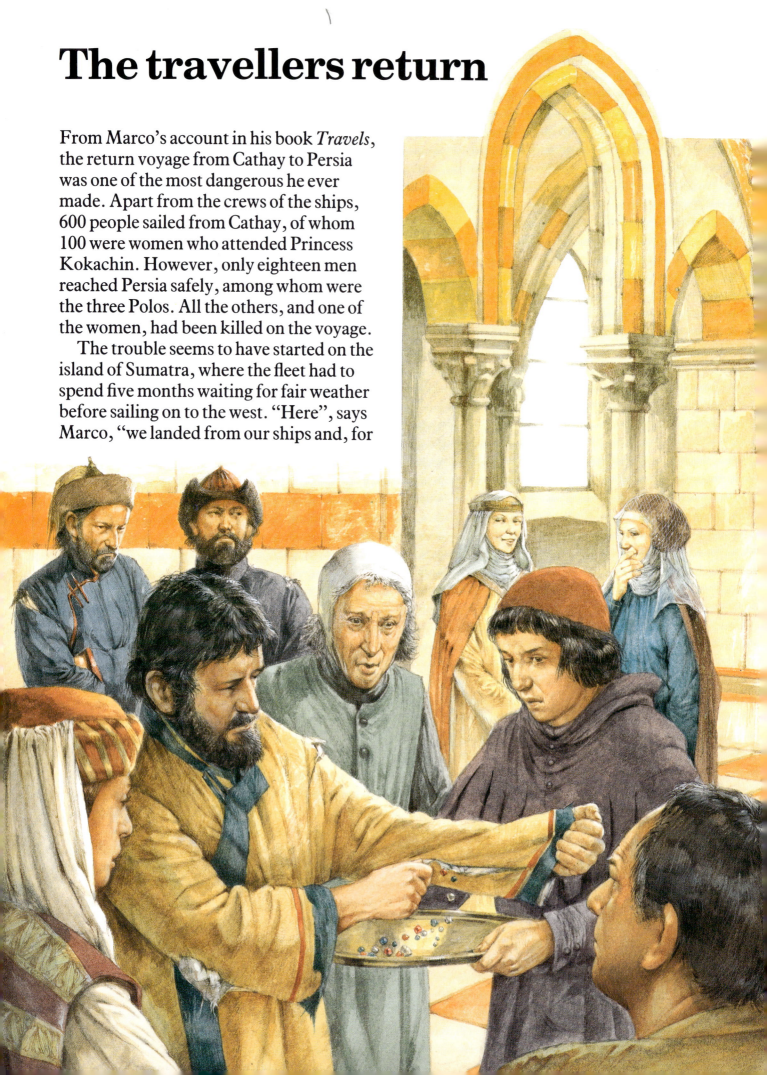

fear of these nasty and brutish people who kill men for food, we dug a big trench round our encampment, extending down to the shore of the harbour at either end. On the embankment of the trench we built five wooden towers or forts; and within these fortifications we lived for five months."

Apart from the obvious dangers which the party faced from the cannibals of Sumatra, Marco mentions other perils encountered during the long sea voyage north up the west coast of India. Here the travellers were repeatedly obliged to fight off attacks by the local inhabitants. "If any ship is driven by stress of weather to put in at any place other than its proper destination, it is seized the moment it comes ashore and robbed of everything on board." Further north, passing the kingdom of Gujarat, today in modern Pakistan, the surviving Cathayan ships had to run the risk of attack by fleets of pirate ships which terrorised merchant shipping along the Indian coast. More than 100 pirate ships set out each year.

At last, eighteen months after leaving Cathay, the Polos and Princess Kokachin landed at the port of Hormuz and headed inland for the court of Arghun Khan, only to find that he had died. Arghun's brother, Kaikhatu, was now Khan of Persia and he gave orders that Kokachin was to be married to Arghun's son, Prince Ghazan. The Princess had become very fond of the Polos after all the dangers they had braved together since leaving Cathay. When the three left her to go back to their own country, she wept to see them go.

The last stage of the homeward journey should have been easy, riding by daily stages to Trebizond on the Black Sea and then home by sea to Venice. But as the Polos reached Trebizond, they were attacked and robbed of most of their hard-earned treasure. They finally arrived back in Venice in the "Year of the Incarnation of Christ, 1295".

As 23 years had passed everybody thought Niccolo, Maffeo and Marco were dead. At first they were turned away from their home as imposters... until they ripped open the seams of their padded clothing, releasing streams of precious jewels.

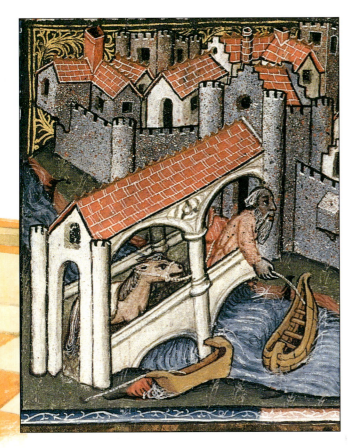

◁ Home at last, the Polos rip open their clothes to release streams of jewels sewn away for safety.

△ The bridge of Sindufu in Tibet which Marco saw, as shown in the "Book of the Great Khan".

"Marco Millions" tells his story

After Marco's dramatic return to Venice in 1295, there was only one other adventure in his life that we know of. This was the sea war between the republics of Venice and Genoa in the years 1296–98. As one of Venice's richest merchants, Marco commanded a war galley in the Battle of Curzola (September 1298), but his luck ran out. The Venetian fleet was defeated and Marco was taken prisoner by the Genoese.

Though Marco could hardly have known it at the time, this was one of the luckiest misfortunes in his life. From Marco's weary months in prison came the book of his adventures, which made him one of the most famous travellers of all time.

It is still astonishing to remember that Marco did not write *Travels* himself. He dictated the book from his amazing memory to a fellow-prisoner, Rustichello of Pisa, who put it into writing. By the time that Marco was released from prison in May, 1299, the book, entitled *Description of the World*, was finished, and it appeared in Venice shortly afterwards. The book became commonly known as *Travels*.

Many Venetians scoffed at Marco as a mere teller of tall stories. They called him *"Il Milione"*, the "millions man". Marco had to live with this nickname until he died in 1324, at the age of 70. He insisted on his death-bed that "I never told the half of what I saw."

Translated into many languages, Marco's *Travels* became one of the most popular books of the Middle Ages. It could even be called one of the most important books in the history of the world. Over 160 years after Marco's death, his description of the riches of Cathay inspired Christopher Columbus to try to reach Cathay by sailing west across the Atlantic Ocean. The result was the discovery of America.

◁ This is Marco Polo's will. Scholars have always wondered why the man who was nicknamed "Marco Millions" by his countrymen did not leave an immense fortune to his family when he died.

▷ Captured in battle and imprisoned by the Genoese, Marco dictates the story of his travels to his cellmate, Rustichello of Pisa. Marco's incredible memory made possible one of the most famous travel books of all time.

Glossary

Caravan Large group of merchants, their servants and animals – camels, horses, and mules – travelling together for maximum safety. The biggest dangers faced by caravans were bandit attacks and long desert crossings. Marco experienced both of these dangers.

Cathay European name for China in the Middle Ages. When Marco reached Cathay in 1274 Kublai Khan's armies had nearly completed the conquest of southern China, driving out the last rulers of the Sung Dynasty. Kublai and his heirs ruled all China as the Yüan Dynasty (1260-1368).

Genghis Khan "Very Mighty Lord": the title taken in 1206 by the Mongol warlord Temujin. He built the Mongol horse-warriors into a mighty army which swept east into northern China and west across Central Asia to southern Russia. Though dreaded for his ferocity in war, he was also a most able ruler.

Karaunas A bandit tribe of Rudbar province in southern Persia, which preyed on merchant caravans passing through the region.

Khan "Lord": a Mongol ruler, elected by the armies. A khan would try to pass

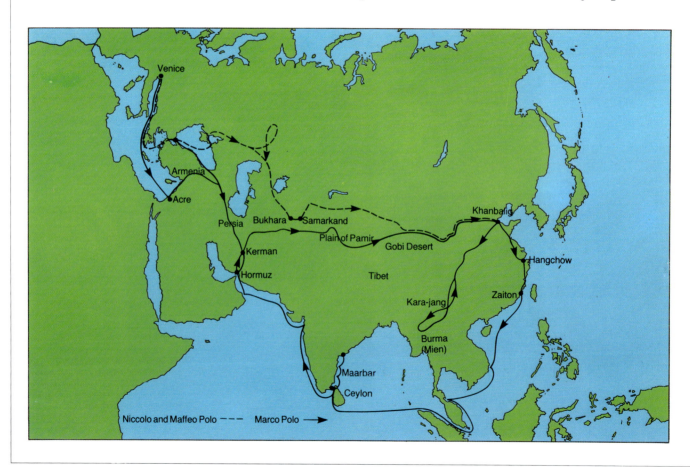

▽ The travels of Marco Polo. The long overland route to Cathay had not been planned by his father and uncle, who had hoped to go most of the way by sea. It was the return journey, after twenty years spent in Cathay, that was made by sea.

Timechart

on his power to his son, but new khans always had to prove their worth as capable generals and rulers. It took a very special leader to be accepted as "Great Khan" by a *kuriltai* or council of the khans.

Khanate A province of the Mongol Empire, ruled by a khan. Outside the Yüan Empire of Mongol China the most important khanates were Turkestan, the "Ilkhanate" of Persia, and the "Khanate of the Golden Horde" in southern Russia.

Kublai Khan Grandson of Genghis Khan; the last and, thanks largely to Marco's account, the most famous of the Mongol "Great Khans", who died in 1294. Kublai's Chinese subjects revered him as the Emperor Shih-tsu.

Mamelukes Warrior-race of Muslim Egypt, and the only people ever to defeat a Mongol invasion (at the Battle of Ain Jalut in 1260). The Mamelukes often raided the western Ilkhanate of Persia, and one of these invasions delayed the Polos' departure for Cathay in 1271.

Mien Mongol name for the Kingdom of Burma, conquered by Kublai Khan and visited by Marco.

Persia Modern Iran; the rich and powerful Muslim kingdom or "Caliphate" conquered by the Mongols under Kublai's younger brother, Hulagu Khan, between 1256 and 1258.

1227 Death of Genghis Khan, founder of the Mongol Empire.
1241 Death of Ogadai Khan saves Europe from conquest by the Mongols.
1254 Marco Polo born in Venice.
1257 Kublai Khan becomes "Great Khan" of the Mongol Empire.
1260–69 Niccolo and Maffeo Polo travel to Cathay and are welcomed by Kublai.
1269 Niccolo and Maffeo return to Venice.
1271 Niccolo, Maffeo and Marco Polo leave Venice for Cathay.
1274 The Polos reach Cathay.
1275–92 Marco's travels through Asia in the service of Kublai.
1293 The Polos and Princess Kokachin sail from Cathay for Persia.
1295 The Polos return to Venice.
1298–99 Marco, captured and imprisoned in Genoa, dictates his *Travels* to Rustichello of Pisa.
1324 Death of Marco, aged 70.
1492–1504 Inspired by Marco's *Travels*, Christopher Columbus makes four Atlantic crossings in search of Cathay, but discovers America instead.

Index

Acre 6
Adam's Peak 21
altitude 11
ambassadors 6
America 28, 31
Arghun 24
Armenia 9
Asia 5, 30, 31
Atlantic 28, 31

Badakhshan 5, 11
bandits 8, 9, 30
Beijing 6
Bengal 21
Black Sea 5, 27
Buddha 20, 21
Buddhism 20
Burma 18, 20, 31

cannibals 27
caravans 9, 12, 13, 30
Cathay 5, 6, 8, 11, 12, 14, 17, 18, 20, 24, 26, 28, 30, 31
Ceylon 20, 21, 22
China 4, 5, 6, 18, 30
Christ 6, 27
Christian Church 6
Christianity 20
Christians 5
Clement IV, Pope 6
Columbus, Christopher 28, 31

Description of the World 28

Egypt 8, 31
Europe 4, 5, 11, 16, 17, 25

Genoa 28, 31
Ghazan, Prince 27

Gobi Desert 12, 13
Gregory X, Pope 8

Hsia-men 25
Holy Land 8
Hormuz 9, 11, 27
Hungary 4

Il Milione 28
Imperial Post 17
India 17, 22, 23, 25, 27
Islam 20
Italy 6

Java 21
Jerusalem 6, 7, 8, 15, 21

Kara-jang 18, 30
Karaunas 9, 30
Kerman 11
khanates 4, 31
Khan 4, 30, 31
Khan, Arghun 27
Khan, Genghis 4, 30, 31
Khan, Hulagu 31
Khan, Kaikhatu 27
Khan, Kublai 4, 5, 6, 7, 8, 14, 15, 16, 18, 30, 31
Khan, Ogadai 4, 31
Khanbalig 6, 21
Kokachin, Princess 24, 26, 31

Maarbar 22, 23
Mamelukes 8, 31
Mediterranean 5, 6
merchants 5, 22, 27, 28, 30
Mien 18, 31
missionaries 5, 6, 8, 15
Mongol Empire 4, 5, 31
Muslim 31

Pagan 18
pagodas 18
Pakistan 27
Palestine 7
Pamir 11, 30
pearls 22, 23
Persia 9, 24, 26, 27, 30, 31
Poland 4
Polo, Maffeo 5, 6, 7, 8, 9, 12, 14, 24, 31
Polo, Niccolo 5, 6, 7, 8, 9, 12, 14, 24, 31

River Balacian 5
River Irrawaddy 18
River Oxus 5
Rome 6
Rudbar 9, 30
Russia 4, 5, 30, 31
Rustichello of Pisa 28, 31

Singapore 21
Sri Lanka 20
Suchow 12
Sudak, Port 4, 5
Sumatra 26, 27

Tamil Nadu 22
Temujin 30
Temur, Essen 18
Tibet 20, 27
trading 5, 23
Travels 9, 14, 26, 28, 31
Trebizond 27
Turkestan 12, 31

Venice 4, 5, 6, 7, 11, 27, 28, 31

Zaiton 5, 25, 30